THE RISKS AND REWARDS
OF THE MODERN MANAGER

The career path of today's manager poses obstacles, dangers, and pitfalls along the way to success and self-realization. Burnout, family and marital problems, substance abuse, and the life-shortening results of stress are but a few of the "dangers to self" faced by a manager. Loss of job and diminished self-esteem through inadequate performance is ever-present as a danger to one on the career path of management.

Your greatest reward and satisfaction as a manager will be from a career that uninterruptedly continues to its highest potential. The resources you will call upon are those from within yourself . . . those that provide the skill and awareness to marshal most productively your resources and those of your organization. This is the path of the Tao.

May the Tao be with you.

BANTAM NEW AGE BOOKS

This important imprint includes books in a variety
of fields and disciplines and deals with the search for
meaning, growth and change.

Ask your bookseller for the books you have missed.

The Tao of Management

An Age Old Study
for New Age Managers

Bob Messing

BANTAM BOOKS

NEW YORK · TORONTO · LONDON · SYDNEY · AUCKLAND

This edition contains the complete text
of the original hardcover edition.
NOT ONE WORD HAS BEEN OMITTED.

TAO OF MANAGEMENT

A Bantam Book / published by arrangement with
Humanics Limited

PRINTING HISTORY
Humanics edition published 1989
Bantam edition / February 1992

Bantam New Age and the accompanying figure design as well as "the search
for meaning, growth and change" are trademarks of Bantam Books,
a division of Bantam Doubleday Dell Publishing Group, Inc.

ISBN 0-553-29505-5

Published simultaneously in the United States and Canada

Bantam Books are published by Bantam Books, a division of Bantam
Doubleday Dell Publishing Group, Inc. Its trademark, consisting of the
words "Bantam Books" and the portrayal of a rooster, is Registered in
U.S. Patent and Trademark Office and in other countries. Marca Registrada.
Bantam Books, 666 Fifth Avenue, New York, New York 10103.

PRINTED IN THE UNITED STATES OF AMERICA

OPM   0   9   8   7   6   5   4   3   2   1

Dedicated to my family, friends, and associates.

Author's Note

Throughout this work, we refer to the manager in the male gender.

No offense or slight is intended or implied to the many female professionals actively and productively engaged in management careers.

Acknowledgment

Special thanks to Gary Wilson, my friend, editor, and publisher. His encouragement, enthusiasm, and plain hard work made this book a reality.

The Titles of the Chapters

Introduction

INTRODUCTION

The Tao Te Ching arrives in the 20th century after more than 4,000 years as a still vibrant body of knowledge and wisdom, amply testified to as being integral to the many "New Age" Tao books offered to the reading public.

I first became acquainted with the I Ching as a young executive/manager through the "sensitivity" and "personal growth" training programs of the 1960's. Those experiences had great impact on me at an intuitive level at that time . . . and even now leave me wondering why so many important things do not really change.

In reacquainting myself with the I Ching, I realized that it's teachings represent great practical value as a guide to the manager . . . that the art and skill of management goes beyond being a "boss" or "leader" . . . that the needs and resources of the 20th century make it possible and necessary for managers at all levels to be productive; to grow effectively; and to realize great satisfaction and material reward from a career path that is also strewn with pitfalls and danger.

Taoism is an ancient mystical teaching that can be traced back about 5,000 years. It emphasizes the harmonious development of physcial, social, and spiritual elements of human life . . . and the self-realization of the whole being in ordinary life.

Tao means "The Way," and *I Ching* or *Te Ching* means "The Book of Change." The I Ching has evolved from the contributions of philosophers through many centuries and the commentaries of scholars through the same period, into a living work of great wisdom and real practical value to a student or to you, a manager.

By accepting and understanding the Way and achieving harmony with universal order, the manager exists in concert with his time and surroundings. A manager is better enabled to enlighten himself and others (associates, subordinates, superiors, government officials, customers, suppliers, to name a few) and accomplish tasks.

We might safely say that the teachings and the Way of the Tao speak directly to management through: 1) receptiveness to reality: 2) unbiased understanding; 3) timing of action and inaction; and 4) avoidance of subjectivity and arbitrariness as basis for action.

To be realistic and practical, management is task-or-result oriented, whether commercial in nature or not. Today's manager is a "change manager" in a society that may be described as overly dependent on and fixated with technology and high rates of change. Therefore, the manager must develop his skills and insights to manage change while influencing its rate, direction, and extent. The path for developing these skills, awarenesses, and insights lies within oneself. For the important matters, a manager is on his own.

The career path of today's manager poses obstacles, dangers, and pitfalls along the way to success and self-realization. Burn-out, family and marital problems, substance abuse, and the life shortening results of stress are but a few of the "dangers to self" faced by a manager. Loss of job and diminished self esteem through inadequate performance is ever present as a danger to one on the career path of management. The Tao enables a manager to tap his inner resources on the way to real success, human accomplishment, and satisfaction.

The Tao cautions against arrogance, materialism, insincerity, self-aggrandizement, i.e., self-serving behaviors and characteristics. As managers, we have all seen these traits in people we consider "successful" and even "heroic," and wonder later why these self-serving behaviors are often so highly rewarded with material success and social acclaim.

The path of the Tao is deeply rooted in ethical behavior. A manager following this path will avoid the rapid rise and fall of the "Flash-in-the-pan" hero. The path of the Tao in management is one of attainment, harmony, and of reaching one's potential. To accomplish these things, the ethical teachings of the Tao allow the manager to clearly establish a working value system in order to avoid the disasters faced by those who manage in a shallow, selfish, and overly forceful manner.

Your greatest reward and satisfaction as a manager will

be from a career that un-interruptedly continues to its highest potential. The resources you will call upon are those from within yourself . . . those which provide the skill and awareness to marshall most productively your resources and those of your organization. This is the path of the Tao.

May the Tao be with you.

The Tao of Management

THE CREATIVE—Ch'ien

1. The Creative

The creative represents the strength of Tao, you, and your organization.

Strength is born, expanded, fulfilled, and consolidated. If any of these aspects of strength are lacking, the creative quality of strength is not complete.

The manager must never confuse strength with force. They are not the same.

The manager concentrates on the accomplishment of his task(s), and is minimally visible.

Arrogance is the extreme of knowing something about winning but nothing about losing. Arrogance blocks a manager by diminishing his creative strength.

RECEPTIVE—K'un

2. Receptive

Receptive is the nature of the man who serves. It is the station of second place. Thusly, should all managers describe themselves.

The manager becomes receptive, yielding, devoted, moderate, and correct.

The receptive mind is obedient to natural principles and is able to develop understanding from confusion.

The manager makes things right, strives for fulfillment of his duty, and completes his tasks without fabrication.

DIFFICULTY AT THE BEGINNING—Chun

3. Difficulty at the Beginning

We all experience difficulty at the beginning. It occurs when the creative and receptive unite to create. This is always and naturally the case.

A manager's success in dealing with difficulty at the beginning is achieved through perseverance, delaying activities, and through the selection of helpers.

The confusion of difficulty will result in order.

The manager pursues goals within a prevailing mood of hesitation and hindrance. He subordinates himself to inferiors so that the hearts of all can be won.

In this case, correctness of management style in dealing with difficulty allows for creativity and results in success.

DARKNESS—Mêng

4. Darkness

Darkness comes from using intellect mistakenly thereby reducing cleverness.

This artificial cleverness results in the seeking of a reality which is already there.

A manager must be open, calm, sincere, and serious. He proceeds along the path of non-contrivance.

The innocence of action needed in the midst of darkness is the innocence which is cognizant of darkness.

Darkness is a confusion which moves the manager on to subsequent enlightenment.

WAITING—Hsü

5. Waiting

Amanager who is sound and strong and able to manage in the midst of danger is "waiting." Waiting is nurturing.

Do not presume upon your supposed strength. Do not hope on the remote chance of luck.

Awareness of danger requires care, caution, the refining of one's self, and the awaiting of the proper time.

When the proper time arrives, after waiting, a manager acts in an appropriate way. A manager is strong and cognitive of danger.

CONTENTION—Sung

6. Contention

Arguments, battles of wit, and issues of right and wrong are behaviors that deviate from harmony. They result in a loss of balance for the manager, the team, and the entire organization.

In following the path of the Tao, the manager becomes acutely aware of his temperament and the nature of that temperament which is most harmful.

Caution and moderation are tempered by inner strength and the holding back of outward aggressiveness. A manager does not seek outside justice.

We all know that winning an argument is not the same thing as getting the job done.

MILITANCY—Shih

7. Militancy

In militancy, the manager chooses the way to punishment and execution, command, and authority . . . and needs the ability to change in order to be effective.

When there is peace, the military manager, even the great military leader, is not needed.

It is not always possible to restore peace in perilous times. Those who disturb and disrupt are often brought forth by forceful management.

A manager in times of militancy proceeds in an orderly manner. Ignorant actions result in casualities and loss of valuable associates and outside allies.

Sometimes, a judicious retreat can avoid mistakes.

When order is restored, there is no longer need for punishment and execution. The manager then rewards meritorious achievement and chastises those of little or no merit.

ACCORD—Pi

8. Accord

A manager must achieve union and accord with what is right and real, and must assure himself inwardly that this accord is based in true reality.

A manager must have an open mind and be willing to give in order to receive. True accord and union with those around you can only come from within.

Further, the manager is known by his associates. Union with ignorant and foolish people will reflect poorly.

True accord calls for leadership. A manager should indeed approach a true leader or teacher. There is nothing wrong with asking for help and/or guidance.

NURTURANCE BY THE SMALL—Hsiao Ch'u

9. Nurturance by the Small

Management from the lower levels is developmental, but can mean small development for the organization and the people in it.

However, a manager who walks with and among his people knows greatness and is humble. A manager grows through humility.

This should represent valuable insight and should be thought over in the spirit of honest self-evaluation.

TREADING—Lü

10. Treading

Treading means forward progress.

A manager needs firmness of purpose here and must operate with strength of mind, robust energy, and sincerity.

In treading, avoid impetuous action because ignorance and incompetence can only bring misfortune.

A manager practices self-mastery in times of peril.

TRANQUILITY—T'ai

11. Tranquility

Tranquility is harmony.

This is developmental in that the small goes and the great comes, and the organization goes through in harmony. There is proper timing in the course of work.

Proper timing in taking advantage of opportunity can bring about tranquility.

Tranquility can be lost by softness. The balanced and flexible manager can bring opposition into submission. Manage strongly while acting in a docile manner so as to nurture your strength widely.

A primary goal for managers is to bring about harmony and to preserve it.

OBSTRUCTION—P'i

12. Obstruction

Obstruction always exists in opposition to harmony. Through obstruction the great goes and the small comes.

The manager's goal is to immediately effect balance. Hiding embarrassment or just being unaware means that the manager does not know that there is obstruction or blockage in the organization.

In times of organizational or individual blockage, it is helpful and even necessary to go back and start over. The manager reverses the flow of events and restores tranquility.

The manager had better be aware of the path of events around him.

FELLOWSHIP AND ASSIMILATION—T'ung Jên

13. Fellowship and Assimilation

Fellowship and assimilation are brought out by the character of the manager, not by his position.

A manager must skillfully and sincerely mix and assimilate with others. This true sameness with others is developmental.

Do not be a fair weather fellow. Be true in good times and in bad.

The manager must always recognize that there are people with whom he should not assimilate. Assimilation as a management technique is based upon correctness and other rational factors, never on emotion.

True mutuality exists as a result of truly natural and productive activity. The manager develops himself inwardly while at the same time developing others outwardly.

This is the condition within which the manager is able to adapt to change and to set truly significant goals.

GREAT POSSESSIONS—Ta Yu

14. Great Possessions

Great possessions represent the success and reward brought about through management efforts and effective work.

The manager must be firm and flexible, in so that which is great, now will grow greater. The manager always builds on strength.

This individual and organizational condition requires nurturing within and the repudiation of adornments.

Daily rewards call for daily renewal by the manager.

HUMILITY—Ch'ien

15. Humility

Humility is having great possessions and not dwelling upon them.

Lacking humility, a manager and his organization become empty, disrespectful, and lazy.

Humility is recognized by its quality and endurance. It should be practiced in both favorable and unfavorable situations.

True humility enriches all. Satiety brings on resentment.

The manager humbly follows the strong, is hard working, and extends his humility to the high and to the low.

Do not underrate the positive effect of true humility.

JOY AND ENTHUSIASM—Yü

16. Joy and Enthusiasm

Joy results from the possession of something great when there is humility.

No manager should be foolish enough in his rejoicing to associate with petty people. Joy in the organization can lead to inertia.

A manager pursues his own true path and not his personal likes. He is in accord with the Tao lest joy be lost.

This joy of gain is achieved through the manager's use of firm strength.

FOLLOWING—Sui

17. Following

Following is developmental. Others rejoice when one acts. The manager is fulfilling the expectations of others.

By following along the path of what is desired, the manager has the opportunity of gradually introducing guidance. He identifies time for action and stillness, and other times for advance and withdrawal. It should not be necessary to remind one that following requires great care in the beginning.

Weak following results in a loss of reality, and then a loss in everything else. Following can result in strength only by abiding in right and not moving . . . and by following while trusting in goodness.

As a manager it is unreasonable to expect others to follow you before you have followed them.

The Tao cautions against ignorance and excess.

DEGENERATION—Ku

18. Degeneration

The manager encounters degeneration following joy and enthusiasm and knows that human and organizational degeneration are preconditions for repair.

The manager returns to fundamentals from which the path of repair will follow. He knows that action will be called for, since degeneration cannot be corrected in a setting of empty tranquiltiy.

This action places the manager in a setting of danger and difficulty. He must not be excessively adamant or weak in correction . . . and he had better know whether things are degenerate or not.

Often, this is the time to utilize the strength and clarity of others to break down one's own ignorance and restore things to a state of no degeneration.

Fame and profit are not your targets here. Spiritual values and virtues allow for no degeneration.

Great progress for the manager and his organization results from dealing effectively with degeneration.

SUPERVISING—Lin

19. Supervising

Supervising is the heart and the core of managing.

Supervising is both creative and developmental wherein the process becomes increasingly manifest and expanding. All systems are "go," and negative factors are repressed.

The manager avoids negligence and eagerness. He identifies appropriate opportunities and takes advantage of them in a correct manner. When supervision is creative and developmental there is no obstruction.

Do not look for "quick fixes." Moving ahead too quickly results in sudden regression.

A manager always seeks guidance and help. Supervision is an ultimate expression of management and the result is completion of both the beginning and the end.

OBSERVING—Kuan

20. Observing

The manager is always an alert and careful observer.

Observation requires clarity of mind and is closely related to degeneration. Alert observation is the path for correcting degeneration.

Sincerity will gain the manager acceptance and success. Inward truthfulness dissipates acquired influences.

Receptiveness and quick action rely on management's skills and observation. Do not accept the false and reject the real.

This is a time for the manager to examine his own growth and the growth of others. Build upon strength.

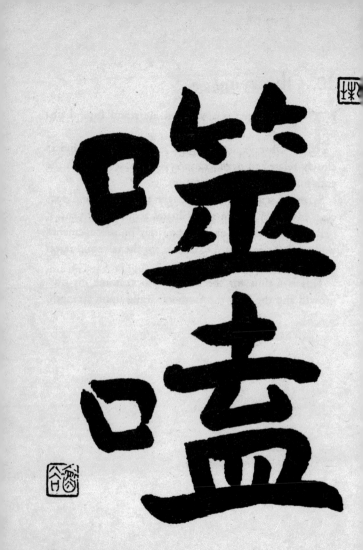

DECISIVENESS—Shih Ho

21. Decisiveness

Decisiveness is acting with unfailing clarity and clear understanding. It is good managing.

A manager can only practice what he clearly and thoroughly understands. The quality of actions is based on understanding.

Decisiveness is "biting through" the entirety of a situation and not "nibbling" around the edges or just "pulling off" what is loose around the bone.

Decisiveness requires and demands true understanding. The manager disregards falsehood and keeps truth.

ADORNMENT—Pi

22. Adornment

Adornment represents beautification.

In managing through observing, we arrive at a condition wherein clarity becomes stabilized. Clarity and stillness adorn each other. A manager does not let stillness degenerate into quietism.

The manager values clarity as a place of rest and stillness. He does not use it lightly as the clarity of illumination. Adornment itself is developmental but results in progress when not overdone.

The manager expands knowledge and wisdom at this time. He shuts out external artifice and does not allow adornment and luxuriance to hinder clarity of understanding.

Real adornment is the mutuality of clarity and stillness, and is a means by which the work of hidden cultivation and quiet practice is not clouded.

STRIPPING AWAY—Po

23. Stripping Away

Stripping away is disposing of everything and thereby having nothing left.

The manager who follows his desires and can only press forward and cannot step back winds up losing basic essence. Eating the fruit and throwing away the pit causes disaster.

While stripping away is most easily described in material and financial terms, its greatest impact to the manager is in the human and spiritual areas.

RETURN—Fu

24. Return

Return means coming back and is developmental. It is necessary to know the timing of the return, not to forcibly seek return at the wrong time, and definitely not to miss a timely opportunity.

The manager must pay close attention to return since it necessitates pursuing work in an orderly fashion. Good must be restored gradually because immediate restoration is inherently unstable.

While return is always possible for the manager and his organization, it is hindered when one is deceived by personal desires and confused by outside influences.

There is great growth for the manager in return but one must be careful in the beginning.

Unstable return requires repetition. The single-minded manager moves through perilous times and returns many times.

This last has to do with the manager learning, losing, and striving diligently.

FIDELITY—Wu Wang

25. Fidelity

A manager conducts himself with whole-hearted sincerity—is creative and developmental without duplicity.

Fidelity is genuine. The manager puts aside external influences while acting in a timely manner, utilizing the appropriate strength.

Do not follow the contrivances of your mind and wrongfully seek treasure. You must give before you can receive.

The benefits of true fidelity can be great . . . and so also can be the misfortunes.

NURTURANCE OF THE GREAT—Ta Ch'u

26. Nurturance of the Great

The manager nurtures and develops his restored energy to make it greater, and more indestructible and incorruptible. One's strength is stilled while on this path so that it can be nurtured and grow.

This is a path without force. Greatness of nurturance results in great development.

Strength is balanced, stabilized, and developed to its highest level, a level of consummation. Improperly promoted strength brings misfortune here. Strength is to be nurtured at the beginning.

A manager treads this path with single-mindedness and a full, complete spirit.

NOURISHMENT—I

27. Nourishment

In nourishment, action and stillness become unified. The manager chooses and holds fast to the good, and seeks fulfillment through emptiness.

Inwardly observing truth and falseness, the manager nourishes the right and is rid of the wrong.

Nourishment, like fulfillment, must be sought by a manager looking inwardly, emptying his mind of irrelevant things.

Be careful in the beginning . . . do not act in ignorance or be distracted by human desire and folly.

EXCESS—Ta Kuo

28. Excess

The manager must be careful in dealing with excess and not indulge in it.

For instance, great strength can do great damage when used to excess. The damage will accrue to the practitioner. Avoid the excessive use of strength by knowing how and when to withdraw.

Excessive weakness is as bad as excessive strength. Harmony, adaptibility, avoiding danger, and being aware of perils imbue the manager with the firmness and flexibility to avoid excess.

Excess of the great can never be one-sided or partial. The manager will do well to recognize this so as not to directly or indirectly call great misfortune on himself.

PITFALLS—K'An

29. Pitfalls

Pitfalls are danger. A manager must know how to get through danger. The path of practice is followed . . . it is the practice of good because good is the way out of danger.

In order to remove onself from danger, one must believe in the danger. Belief rules the mind of the manager. This belief avoids distraction and allows the practice of good.

There is great simplicity in the belief in danger and the need for practice to get out of danger. This is developmental and of great benefit to the manager and his organization.

A manager who repeats pitfalls and continually lives in peril is self-destructive.

FIRE—Li

30. Fire

Fire is cleansing, illuminating, and beneficial for correctness and development.

A manager's development is assisted by fire only if the use and nurturing of its illumination is known. It is the inner illumination referred to here which is the basis for other illumination.

Illumination (inner and outer) results in open awareness, clarity, and action in the path of good. Illuminated work is correct and results in good fortune. The manager must seek illumination constantly in order to use it.

When not illuminated, the manager is aware and seeks illumination from others. This opens the mind, produces understanding, and turns weakness into strength.

Nurture illumination to avoid trouble arising from excess.

The manager who only deals with outer illumination becomes weak, incapable, and impotent of action. From a management point of view, knowing one is not illumined is reparable.

SENSITIVITY—Hsien

31. Sensitivity

Sensitivity means feeling and influence. It represents harmony. The path of sensitivity has the potential of being equally developmental or perilous.

The manager must move with true spontanaity, and ignore outside influence and human desires. Failure to achieve a genuine condition of sensitivity results in humiliation.

Clever words and external artificialities do not represent true sensitivity.

CONSTANCY—Hêng

32. Constancy

Constancy has to do with long persistence and genuine application. It is sound management practice.

While fire involves inward and outward illumining aimed at profound attainment of personal realization, constancy orients the manager toward the single-minded application of the will. The manager is not lazy and does not slack off.

This can be a strong and positive path of development.

We all see managers and associates who are capable of constancy but are constant along deviant paths. They seek success in this manner, but rather hasten their personal and professional demise.

Correct constancy moves the manager to thoroughly penetrate different kinds of truths.

This is a path of action for the manager . . . for without action there is no constancy. Empty evaluation and self-aggrandizement is inevitably followed by ruin, as the culmination of elevation is inevitably followed by a fall.

Fooling oneself is poor management practice and is not the path of the Tao.

WITHDRAWAL—Tun

33. Withdrawal

The manager withdraws when he retracts, using strength with restraint. This is developmental for the manager and keeps external influences from wasting energy.

Care in the beginning is yet again cautioned by the Tao.

Avoid personal entanglements by not acting arbitrarily. The manager subdues energy and accepts the truth.

This is a path where strength and flexibility act equally allowing the manager freedom and independence. This is an individual management choice.

GREAT POWER—Ta Chuang

34. Great Power

Great power is ceaseless internal strength and efficacy in action. This is why it is called great power.

The manager with great power experiences extraordinary direction in life and does what others cannot do. He transcends the ordinary and accomplishes the rare.

Deviation from the path of reality (of Tao), ignorance of danger, and avoidance of change can result in the harming of life by power. There is then no value in power.

The manager who follows this path without care and prudence at the beginning risks the consequences of failure, danger, and peril.

Great power must be kept in balance by the fortunate manager who possesses it. Self-mastery allows this manager to have inwardly more than enough strength and to be powerful without being excessively so.

Weakness without firm strength makes it impossible for the manager (or the organization) to be vigorous even though the time and situation call for vigor. The weak and incapable seek a teacher.

Studying, practicing, and working intensely while struggling intensely is becoming powerful by resorting to what is right.

The path of Tao . . . virtue and correctness lead to the achievement of great power.

ADVANCE—Chin

35. Advance

Advance is management progress which is based on understanding and growing illumination.

The manager restores illumination to the darkness of the closed mind through obedience, timing, and truth.

Seek illumination when it is not advanced and do not rush to promote it in the midst of darkness. Seek the illumination of others, when necessary.

The manager is secure when he is in a state of tranquility and peace. There is no management situation where one cannot use illumination and there is no place that can damage true illumination.

明
月
夷

CONCEALMENT OF ILLUMINATION—Ming I

36. Concealment of Illumination

Where being strong in action results in advance without withdrawal, power is excessive, injures the manager's illumination, and ruins power.

The manager conceals not his illumination in a most secret place and does not use it lightly. Concealment and the nurturing of inward and outward illumination allows it to be free of defect.

When illumination does not penetrate reality, injury is caused.

This injury causes the manager to withdraw and conceal the illumination. Outward hurt does not mean inward hurt. Withdraw and conceal illumination when damage is suffered.

This is the "damage—control" of the Tao and is good management practice.

Illumination is to be nurtured, stored, and available.

INNER GOVERNANCE—Chia Jên

37. Inner Governance

The manager refines himself, masters his mind, and turns his attention around to gaze inward.

By not being firm in refinement, the manager allows laziness, trickiness, and self-indulgence to destroy order. He is humiliated.

Balance here unifies firmness and flexibility and allows one to seek out and pursue the path of gentility toward a purpose of selflessness.

Self-governance, selflessness, and the refinement of the inner self is a serious matter.

DISHARMONY—K'uei

38. Disharmony

All managers face mutual opposition and know that it is best settled when it first arises. It also can be settled correctly when it is in full force.

The manager must bring union from disharmony. The mind must restore the light from within. When this is done and desires are swept away and feelings are forgotten, it is possible to reconcile disharmony.

Disharmony can be caused by oneself where no disharmony has existed. The manager damages the inward by striving for the outward, by accepting the false. There is an end but no beginning. Regret is useful in settling disharmony only if you regret in the beginning and at the end.

Take care with whom you associate. Associate with the right people because there is disharmony in solitude. Do not manage in a vacuum.

Most importantly, settle disharmony in the open, take advantage of timing, and use the settlement of small matters to correct disharmony in large ones.

In managing, take care of the small things, but settle the large matters as well since they will not take care of themselves.

HALTING—Chien

39. Halting

A manager halts. He stops in the midst of danger. Forward progress is difficult here because the extreme of danger has burdened the inner mind with external influence. Halting allows the manager to deal with and leave danger.

The manager controls danger by stillness and solves danger by action. Stillness and action are both functions of the mind of Tao.

The manager is careful in halting when weakness is present. Seeking guidance from others and forming associations with correct people broadens the manager's knowledge and wisdom.

The manager is best counseled to follow the Tao by being firm and not getting into trouble in the first place.

LIBERATION AND FREEDOM—Hsieh

40. Liberation and Freedom

Sound management practice calls for taking advantage of the right time.

Returning without going anywhere does not come about through human effort. It appears spontaneously at a given time and comes from nature. When nature's time arrives, however, human exertion is necessary.

The manager must use inner resources to be liberated from danger and difficulty . . . and to be able to act freely as he wants. While promptness brings good fortune, tardiness here will result in failure.

Liberation can be achieved regardless of one's condition. When weak and helpless, and danger is extreme, associate with the right people and borrow their strength.

Adamance alone does not create sufficient force to liberate. Being strong will not do the job where weakness is present. The balance between looseness and tightness is the liberation of Tao which sublimates all difficulty.

Timing, knowledge, illumination, and true recognition make the difference between management success and failure.

REDUCTION—Sun

41. Reduction

A manager diminishes that which is excessive, thereby increasing accomplishment.

Practically speaking, there are few more important things to a manager than finishing those tasks which he starts.

This is a very positive and subtle practice in management. Wrath, cupidity, and other disruptive conditions eat away at the natural reality of task and goals.

To practice reduction on a daily basis is to increase daily accomplishment.

Care at the beginning, conscientious reduction, and sincerity result in spontaneous increase in strength and perfection of beginning and end.

INCREASE—I

42. Increase

Effective management adds to and augments what is lacking on both individual and organizational levels.

The goal here is to eliminate compulsive habits. This constitutes management of self. Increasing through reduction the fundamental management process of constant beginnings and conclusions.

There is no need here to elaborate on the effect of beginnings without endings, or of the risk and peril of assisting others before developing oneself. Management is always "self-management" first.

"Do as I say—Not as I do" is not the path of the Tao.

PARTING—Kuai

43. Parting

The manager separates himself from mundanity.

The temporal conditioning for wine, sex, and the trappings of wealth are confusing to those who *must* rule their own minds. The human mind likes these things.

A deep understanding of process, flexibility, and timing will gradually dispose of the aggregate of mundanity. Spontaneous illumination shortly follows.

The manager should avoid excessive force. Parting is a natural process where reason prevails over authority.

Impetuosity must give way to a path that travels between intensity and laxity.

A final warning: be alert and wary. Do not allow mundanities to catch you by surprise.

MEETING—Kou

44. Meeting

We have all observed the manager who is not mindful . . . who sits by and watches mundanity (even indulges it) and cannot prevent it.

Mundanity and obstacles are encountered constantly. The manager who follows the path of the Tao wards them off as they are met.

The energy of the mundane is negative and acts as a brake. It stops everything and is exceedingly difficult to subdue.

One definition of arrogance would be a manager's tardiness in warding off mundanity.

GATHERING—Ts'ui

45. Gathering

The developmental benefit of the manager gathering what is right is far reaching.

This concentrates vitality and energy. The manager who corrects himself and others can truly be described as a great person.

It is the foolish manager who watches time go by, and then openly and loudly regrets an ending of misfortune. This can also be described as carelessness in the beginning.

Since not all (or many) managers are great persons, the weak, incapable, and ordinary manager can experience joy, enlightenment, and accomplishment by borrowing the strength and wisdom of others.

RISING—Shêng

46. Rising

Management development can be accurately described as a climbing from lowness to highness. It is also a meaningful goal for both the manager and his organization. Rising is developmental in the extreme, and is a gradual and orderly path.

Learning from those who can teach and avoiding blind practice offers the manager a clear path of accomplishment without obstacles or obstruction.

Ignorance, arbitrary action, and vain imaginings of growth result in a rising into darkness, not into illumination. It is the teacher's wisdom that restores self-realization as if it were always there.

This is a clear statement of a primary management development goal. Avoid complacency, self-satisfaction, and false joy.

EXHAUSTION—K'un

47. Exhaustion

Managing is no exception to the phenomenon of exhaustion. It is an unavoidable impasse faced continually by all individuals and organizations.

The fair-weather manager blames others and complains. His main concern is usually the material. An exhausted body, however, can resolve impasse if the mind (the inner self) is not exhausted.

Accomplishment and success after hardship cannot be achieved immediately. Gradual growth is required after exhaustion.

As in many management pitfalls and obstacles, ignorant and arbitrary action create yet more exhaustion and is self-destructive. A manager seeks harmonious progress.

THE WELL—Ching

48. The Well

Every manager is deeply involved in the development of others such as subordinates, associates, even superiors.

It should be simply said, however, that the most important development project for the manager is his self-development. This is a precondition to the development of others.

To attempt the development of others before attaining one's own goals will always result in *not* helping others and also losing oneself.

On the other hand, developing others through self-development, nurtures others and oneself, and represents real achievement for the organization.

Self-development is the true basis for an inexhaustible source of nourishment and development for all.

RIDDANCE—Ko

49. Riddance

Every manager must get rid of his ego to move along a path of development and creativity.

Of equal importance to the manager is the riddance of personal desires from his inner self. This will eliminate obsolescent traits, and transform him and his organization.

Riddance is the non-striving revolution of the great person. He is then able to reform others and his organization.

Sincerity, selflessness, and illumined strength are to be strived for by the manager and those around him.

REFINED HEATING—Ting

50. Refined Heating

In self-development, the manager achieves illumination and then refines this by following an initiatory process that solidifies his life and strength.

This process is developmental and good. The refining process and procedure must be followed diligently. The manager cannot deviate.

Discard the old, comprehend essence and life, and anticipate peril. Spontaneous illumination will burn away acquired mundanity.

Illumination is promoted slowly, according to process, and carefully overseen.

ACTION—Chên

51. Action

The essence and expression of management is action. More clearly, it is continuous action within which the manager pursues his own development.

In the midst of constantly repeated action, the inner activity of inward thoughts establishes the quality of the outer activity called worldly affairs.

The manager follows the path of the Tao . . . of inner clarity and consistency of thought . . . nurtures his energy and contributes genuine activity with no impediment to action.

In weakness, borrow the strength of others. Be wary, especially of our own weakness.

The path of action of the Tao is unaffected by ups and downs.

STILLNESS/STOPPING—Kên

52. Stillness/Stopping

By stopping, the manager becomes inwardly and outwardly still. In this stopping there is the stillness tested with action. This is not the stillness of inaction.

Stopping in the right place without wavering is a way to test and to learn, alternating between action and inaction.

The manager seeking the path of the Tao and the attainment of self-realization does not allow himself the craving of victory and quick success.

There is no benefit from management through weakness or random speech. Knowing the Tao is knowing when to stop.

GRADUAL PROGRESS—Chien

53. Gradual Progress

The path of the Tao leading to self realization and attainment of goals is a subtle process . . . a long course of work.

Management of oneself and others toward this goal is gradual by nature.

Quick success is not the way of the Tao. A natural and gradual progress, an orderly progress, produces the correct manner of thoroughly investigating truth and completely realizing the essence which arrives at the meaning of life.

Do not be a manager who grows old without achievement.

歸

妹

INTERCOURSE IS NOT PROPER—Kuei Mei

54. Intercourse is not proper

It is improper to actively seek enjoyment in such a way that behavior obeys emotion.

The manager who follows the Tao does not use emotion to seek essence. This is incorrect and not of the appropriate time.

Use essence to seek feeling. Manage correctly so that enjoyment comes from what can be properly enjoyed.

Be aware of those many occasions when the manager must await proper timing. Manage oneself and others in such a way as to turn back from error.

RICHNESS—Fêng

55. Richness

The manager who achieves illumination and action in concert finds the path of the Tao effortless and clear.

This is the richness truly described by the words *fullness* and *greatness*. This richness is developmental. The manager is effective in his thoughts and actions. Illumination and action are great. Richness has been achieved.

Seek out illumination at the beginning through the guidance of others. Strength produces richness at the beginning.

As in almost all management activities, one does not associate with the wrong people. Here we find that illumination can be blocked rather than increased. This is a management lesson that cannot be learned too well or relearned too often.

Solitary quietude and self-satisfied rest through ignorance are empty richnesses which all managers are well advised to avoid.

The way of the Tao is to achieve richness and presence through attainment and balance. These represent fundamental management values, as do the importance of dealing with all matters adaptively and to depend on oneself, not on fate.

TRAVEL—Lü

56. Travel

Management activity and development can be well described as a course of travel passing through without limping. Illumination is stabilized throughout and not used carelessly.

The path of management is, in a sense, a one-way trip. The manager does not remain unduly attached to the realm(s) through which he passes. This is developmental.

Inward disturbance and outward obscurity do not act on the manager to spoil his trip.

It is not necessary here to dwell on the perils which can be brought on through weakness, lack of clarity, harshness toward others, and simple bad timing and behavior.

The manager in tune with the Tao deals with his world without destroying it, and transcends the world while he is in it.

Enjoy your travels.

FLEXIBILITY AND OBEDIENCE—Sun

57. Flexibility and Obedience

It is not always possible to manage in a climate where mutual understanding and action are unified.

Flexibility and obedience provide for endurance, gradual progress, and penetration. This is the way of the wind. Small but developmental.

The manager is here faced with a real necessity to apply practical steps, make gradual progress, and to continue until the great path is completed.

To follow the path of the Tao, a manager knows when to hurry and when to relax. He knows what will bring good results, and he knows when to stop.

JOY—Tui

58. Joy

Joy is the delight found in managing along the path of the Tao. It allows the practice of Tao. It is developmental.

The manager who finds fulfillment encounters the true reality and essence of joy. Wealth and material gain alone are not the delight of the manager who follows the path of Tao.

What kind of manager do you want to be? Would you prefer to possess the joy of controlled and balanced strength, or would you rather indulge yourself in self-satisfaction and outward appearances?

The Tao speaks clearly as to the correctness of joy.

DISPERSAL—Huan

59. Dispersal

Dispersal means disorganization and disorder, circumstances by now familiar to all who manage.

A fundamental and critically important task for managers is always the reordering of that which is (or has become) dispersed.

Management here follows a path of progress through obedience, of self mastery and returning to appropriate order, with the manager returning to his original being. Paradoxically, this is developmental.

Danger is passed by when management process and behavior follow the path of the Tao and when the manager does not *lose control in situations of great difficulty and stress.*

DISCIPLINE—Chieh

60. Discipline

The manager utilizes discipline to set limits that are not to be exceeded. Every manager faces the need and challenge to practice discipline (and obedience), especially in unfavorable circumstances.

By managing along the path of the Tao, one finds peace wherever he is. Difficulties do not disturb the minds of those who practice reality and delight in the Tao.

Be aware that, even though discipline is developmental, failure to adapt to change and clinging to *one* discipline brings on danger.

We all strive for consistency of movement and adaptability to events. Discipline according to time is an important management goal.

Focus also on the potential and value of peaceful and spontaneous discipline.

A last word: do not use the strength of discipline to court danger in the hope of good luck.

FAITHFULNESS—Chung Fu

61. Faithfulness

Faithfulness is truthfulness from within. This is managing with a balance of inner joy and outer accord.

By being unfaithful to the Tao, the manager risks insubstantial and inadequate power leading to failure in completing tasks.

To practice the Tao only when all is well is to follow the path of mediocrity. It is beneficial to bear up to great obstacles and situations of difficulty and stress.

It is faithfulness to the Tao and correct practice that enable one who manages to perfect essence and life and to complete the beginning and the end.

This is the meaning of effectiveness and a job well done.

PREDOMINANCE OF THE SMALL—Hsiao Kuo

62. Predominance of the Small

Predominance of the small serves to nurture the great.

To manage this developmental process, subtlety and tranquility must be maintained.

In small matters and affairs, the manager adopts a non–striving mode. This is a matter of management versatility, since striving for the great while unable to deal with the small endangers the great. The capability for change-of-pace is an essential management skill.

As a point of guidance, do not dwell too long on the predominance of the small— it is a passing mode, and excess and/or insufficiency should be avoided.

SETTLED—Chi Chi

63. Settled

As illumination and danger, understanding and difficulty offset each other . . . this is called settlement.

To achieve this state the manager forestalls danger, foresees peril, and completes the basis of the elixir in a stable manner.

Settlement is developmental, but arbitrary action and presumption upon illumination cause darkness to come and block the important development of settling.

Use illumination in the beginning to forestall danger. Then even if danger exists, there is no peril. It is always sound practice to prevent danger early on.

At the accomplishment of settlement, dismiss intellectualism and guard against danger.

Timing and balance here result in the comprehension of both essence and life.

NOT YET SETTLED—Wei Chi

64. Not Yet Settled

Managing oneself and others most often takes place in this condition or climate.

Settlement can be achieved when the need for it can be discerned. You must manage toward a goal of settlement. You must want it.

In managing along the path of the Tao, alway investigate the truth and press to seek settlement.

CONCLUSION

This work was conceived to present the teachings of the I Ching as a practical, real life guide to management problems and opportunities.

In pursuing that goal, much of the mysticism, rich imagery, and metaphor of the source material was excluded. It is hoped that a future work may utilize the mystic teachings and practices of the I Ching as a guide and inspiration for the serious management professional.

The interested reader is urged to explore the I Ching. Contemporary translations of several versions are readily available. This "Book of Change" dates back almost 5,000 years and is distinguished amongst the great literature of the world by its secular orientation. It never dealt with religious or political teachings, but rather with quality of life and attainment of self-actualization for the individual living an ordinary life in his own real world.

The wisdom of the I Ching was intended to be of practical use. It's useful and beneficial wisdom and insight for all readers is evidenced by its survival in a still-living form over thousands of years.

The path of the Tao is an elusive, endless, and enriching journey. It is hoped that the serious management professional reading this book has been left with useful insights into himself and his world, as well as some pressing questions having to do with relationships, work, and goals.

Be aware that questions are more important than answers, and that effort, wisdom, and the *quality* of trying are what propels a manager and his organization to meaningful levels of success and accomplishment.

The Tao cautions against quick fixes. The reader should certainly not look upon the Tao as a quick fix to solve real or imagined problems or to achieve what might wrongly be perceived as material or worldly success.

In managing oneself toward success and self-actualization, some guidelines from the Tao deserve extra reflection and consideration. They are:

1) Difficulty and trouble in work and personal activity do not make you different . . . or even unique.
2) Management is a skill process which can, and must, be learned. You can teach yourself, learn from others, or do both.
3) Management is always, to the largest extent, result and/or task oriented.
4) A manager must develop a comfortable, effective, and durable style of both behavior and action.
5) Self-knowledge and real awareness of oneself and surroundings are the foundation upon which a manager builds his repertoire of skills.
6) Simplicity and clarity of form and function are to be strived for and valued.

May the Tao be with you!

Biography

Bob Messing, 50, spent his adult life as a business manager. He worked for both small and large corporations, as well as community, educational, trade, and other organizations. Messing was Chairman and CEO of his own specialty chemical company, and had interests and advisory positions in a number of small businesses. He also served as a Director of Power and Systems Institute (Boston, Massachusetts), and was a founding Advisory Board Member of the Graduate School of Applied and Professional Psychology at Rutgers University (New Brunswick, New Jersey).

About the Artist

The illustrations for this work were commissioned by the Author and are part of his personal collection. This contemporary calligraphy was created by Mr. Quian-Shen Bai, a member of the Taipei Calligraphy and Art Advisory Board, The Calligraphy Association of China in Beijing, and a founding member of the Conglang Calligraphy Club in Suzhou. He is the author of several published commentaries on Classic Calligraphy, in addition to being a contributor to Beijing's History and Theory of Fine Arts Quarterly.